905

WOMEN AND WAR

FIONA REYNOLDSON

Wayland

WOMEN AND WAR

Titles in this series

Aftermath of War   **Victims of War**
Propaganda   **World Leader**
Technology of War   **Women's War**

Cover illustration: A 1944 Soviet poster shows a woman helping to rebuild Leningrad after the German attempt to capture the city.

First published in 1993 by
Wayland (Publishers) Limited
61 Western Road, Hove
East Sussex BN3 1JD, England

© Copyright 1993 Wayland (Publishers) Limited

Series editor: Paul Mason
Designer: John Yates

British Library Cataloguing in Publication Data
    Reynoldson, Fiona
    Women's War – (Era of the Second
    World War)
    I. Title II. Series
    940.53

ISBN 0-7502-0785-X

Typeset in the UK by Dorchester Typesetting Group
Printed and bound in Italy by Rotolito Lombarda S.p.A.

Picture acknowledgements
Archiv fur Kunst und Geschichte 4, 9, 10, 13, 16, 17, 19, 20, 28, 29, 31, 32, 33, 36, 39, 40, 41; Camera Press 26, 30; Imperial War Museum 7, 38; Popperfoto 6, 8, 11, 14 both, 18, 22, 23, 24, 35, 42, 43, 44; Topham title page, 12, 15, 27, 37; Wayland Picture Library 5, 25.

Contents

Introduction

Because history – especially the history of war – has usually been written by men about men's activities, very little has been written about women's experience of war. Yet during the Second World War women made up half the world population, and the war was a truly world-wide one. It directly affected women as well as men. The invention of bombing from aeroplanes brought devastation and death to the home front, far

This 1942 US poster asking people to buy war bonds shows a woman at home with her daughter. But by the end of the war, hundreds of thousands of women everywhere had worked and fought outside the home as resistance fighters, members of the armed forces, factory workers and farmers, among other jobs.

"**Even a little can help a lot - NOW**"

Buy
U.S. WAR STAMPS BONDS

ILLUSTRATION COURTESY OF LADIES' HOME JOURNAL

behind the battle lines. The fighting took place over large areas of the globe, so many homes were burnt down or blown to pieces. Farms, shops, offices, villages, towns and cities were destroyed as huge armies swept across the land.

The scale of the war meant that every pair of hands was needed: more women than ever before were called on. Women were not only needed to nurse, cook and wash laundry for the soldiers (those jobs were not new), but also to build aeroplanes, ships and guns while the men went to fight. Women sometimes picked up the guns and fought the enemy themselves.

FOOD

The war was so large-scale that enormous amounts of food and other goods were needed by the men fighting it. (There were twelve million men in the US forces by 1945.) Rationing (the sharing out of food, petrol, clothes etc.) was introduced in many countries. There were shortages of everything from butter and coffee to leather and nylon. Men **and** women suffered, but it was most often the women on whom the main job of feeding and clothing families fell. It was women who carried the brunt of making do from day to day. How to get food, cook it and preserve it, and how wonderful it was to have it at all, dominated the thoughts of women around the world.

LOVED ONES

Very often women were separated from husbands, boyfriends, brothers and fathers, and worried terribly over whether they would return from the fighting. Often there was grief over their death or injury. Another worry was over children – how to save them, care for them, feed them and educate them.

OPPORTUNITIES

There is no doubt that the war brought tremendous suffering and hardship to women as well as to men. But some women were luckier. Some found in war an opportunity for independence that they had never

JOIN THE ATS

ASK FOR INFORMATION AT THE NEAREST EMPLOYMENT EXCHANGE OR AT ANY ARMY OR ATS RECRUITING CE

Many posters aimed to encourage women to join the armed services. The use of this one was questioned because it made joining the ATS look too glamorous.

5

Women sitting in the rubble of their home in London in 1940.

Charity Adams was in Paris just after it was liberated and saw the joy and celebration of the French women and men on the streets: 'In Paris itself the streets were crammed with people. From the moment we stepped off the train, everyone in US military uniform was subject to the victory hysteria of the French. We were kissed, offered drinks, asked for souvenirs. If you had none, they were taken. You lost your cap, badges, epaulettes, even the braid on your sleeve.'[2]

dreamt of before. When the war came, women were wanted in all sorts of jobs. Governments pleaded for women to join the war effort. Work outside the home was available to women for the first time. There was even a choice of jobs. *'I thought about the Land Army, but then I thought about picking sprouts with the frost on them – so on second thoughts I joined the WRENS.'* (Mrs Swiss)[1]

'All the girls wanted to go into the WRENS – that super uniform. I had never been further than Colwyn Bay and eventually I ended up in Malaya. It was wonderful.' (Mrs Rogerson)[1a]

In Britain and the USA, opportunities beckoned. Charity Adams joined the US Women's Army Corps in 1942 and was the first black woman to be made an officer. She became commanding officer of the only black women's organization posted overseas. This was the 6888th Central Postal Directory, which dealt with US soldiers' mail in Europe. She faced problems over prejudice against black people as well as prejudice against women, but she overcame them all.

Why aren't there many accounts about women's part in the war? There seem to be a number of reasons. One is that in many parts of the world women had a very subservient position. No one asked for their opinion. Few women would have thought that their opinion or their experiences of war were worth talking or writing about. War was men's business. Women's business was to have children, mind the home and work in the fields. Often women could not read or write: it is very hard to find written accounts of the experiences of Burmese and Malayan women during the war.

Many women wanted to go home and forget about the war. This was often so with Soviet women, but it was not the only reason for so little being written by them. Although Soviet women took a larger part in combat than those of any other country, it was still considered to be very unwomanly. The women who had fought at the front wanted to go home and get married. Many said later that they had hidden their

wartime service so they would not be scorned and rejected. A few outstanding women were decorated with medals and honoured as heroes, but most went back to ordinary life and were forgotten.

In the West the picture was different in some ways. In the USA and Europe women were far better educated than in the East. They were used to a more independent life. Some worked at skilled jobs; they were teachers, nurses, civil servants and business women. They were articulate. They knew they had had experiences that would interest other people, so more books and accounts were written. There was more money in the West to buy books and to make television and radio programmes about all sorts of things to do with the war. Therefore it is not as difficult to find accounts of German, French, British, US and Australian women. Even so they are far outnumbered by the accounts by men.

Finally, some women's experiences – of rape, unwanted pregnancy or forced prostitution – were so terrible that they were ashamed to tell even their closest friends. They certainly did not want to write about these experiences.

Jadwiga Pilsudska escaped from Poland with her mother in 1939. She was already an experienced pilot and ferried planes in Britain during the war.

Evacuation

People ran away from the places where soldiers were fighting. They ran away from places that were bombed. This happened all over the world. Sometimes the running away or evacuation was well planned: sometimes it was not organized at all.

THE THREAT OF THE BOMBERS

Britain was one of the first countries to plan evacuation. If its cities were bombed they could be destroyed. The British government organized trains to run from London and other cities to safe places in the country. About three million children were evacuated in September 1939. Many, many mothers stood on railway stations waving goodbye to their children. They knew the war would be terrible, but they did not know if they would ever see their children again. The French and Germans also ran evacuation trains from their big cities. Like the British they were afraid of bombing. Thus all over Europe in 1939, women faced the beginnings of the agony of war – separation from their children, their loved ones or their homes. There were other organized evacuations too.

In 1944 the US started to bomb Japanese cities. The Japanese quickly organized the evacuation of 400,000 children to the country.

THE THREAT OF INVASION

Women and children in the USSR were evacuated when the Germans invaded the USSR. Olga and Zinaida Vasilyevna were evacuated with their mother in 1942. The bombing had already started: *'Our town was being bombed and everything was burning. The order was given to evacuate. We travelled for days until we reached Stalingrad. Women and children were moving to the rear. The men were going the opposite way – to the front. They shouted to us: "Mothers and sisters, get the harvest in for us. Look after our homes." But what could we do? We had only the clothes we stood up in'.*[3]

The French, like the British, organized evacuation at the beginning of the war. Thousands of people moved from the north-east of France. The government knew that the Germans might invade, and they wanted to clear the area so that the French soldiers had room to fight off the Germans. The writer Somerset Maugham watched the evacuation. He remembered looking in the window of a cake shop. All the cakes had gone mouldy. The woman who ran the shop had been forced to leave so quickly that she had no time to take the cakes with her, or even to give them away.

German women aboard a train in 1940. At the start of the war Britain, France and Germany all organized evacuations of civilians from big cities because they feared bombing or invasion.

London was by far the largest city in Britain. The London County Council made detailed plans to evacuate the city. London was divided into six areas. Each area was based around one or two of the big London stations. The whole of Britain was divided into three types of areas: evacuation, neutral and reception areas.

The idea was to move mothers with children under five years of age, children over five, pregnant women and disabled people away from the evacuation areas. One and a half million people were moved in a week around the start of September 1939 by the government. Two million more people arranged their own evacuations.

A ship crowded with German refugees fleeing from the east as Soviet forces invaded in 1945. The refugees have had to leave their possessions behind.

Very often the fighting was so near that there was no time to organize trains, trucks or anything else. In 1937 the Chinese fled as the Japanese invaded their country. 'Families fleeing from war areas usually have four or five children. They have to travel vast distances. Transport is so difficult we hear little children cry, "Father, Mother, do not leave me behind. I won't cry any more." Often, soon only one or two are left. Their mothers have no money or strength . . .'4

By the end of the war Germany was exhausted and defeated. But ships were organized to take people across the Baltic Sea away from the invading Soviets. In the terrible winter of 1945, children pulled their sick mothers on sledges through the snow to reach the ships. Desperate mothers who could not get a place on a ship threw their babies into the arms of people on board to try and save their children.

As the war went on year after year, more and more women around the world were affected by it. In 1945 the USA had been fighting the Japanese for over three years. Slowly, the US army moved closer to Japan. The Americans decided to bomb Japanese cities: in March 1945, 250 B-29 bombers dropped 2,000 tonnes of fire bombs on Tokyo. This was the start of many more fire-bomb raids on Japanese cities. The traditional Japanese bamboo and wooden houses went up in sheets of flames. Thousands of people died in shelters, in the streets or in the canals (where they had tried to escape the fierce heat). Many of those who survived the bombing fled to the country. They joined thousands of others trying to grow rice on the hills around the cities. There was not enough food for everyone, and many starved.

Other Japanese were fleeing from the US forces advancing in the Philippines; still others fled from the Soviets advancing in Manchuria. Chiaru Kono was one among many women who lost her husband in Manchuria and had to get away from the fighting with her children: '*The Russian tanks were on their way. We dashed frantically for the hills as the railway station was blown up. It was 15 August 1945, the day the war ended, that we started out on our death march. We had to keep clear of roads and keep in the hills. There was nothing to eat. No matter how hard I squeezed my breasts there was no milk for my baby. I moistened some of our precious canned bread to give to him. The other children had to gnaw raw potatoes and roots. We could not keep up with the others so we fell behind and slept huddled together in the mountains. I determined not to die before my children and leave them helpless. They never complained.*

'*On the night of 27 August, we lay down on the top of a low hill. The air was full of mosquitoes. I had the children sleep face to face as I kept watch. For a long time Isao, my third son, could not sleep. He kept asking for water. In the morning everyone got up but him. He was dead. We could not bury him so I covered him with some cotton trousers and we picked wild flowers for him. Then, torn with grief, we had to go on.*

The Japanese city of Hiroshima after an atomic bomb had been dropped on it in 1945. At the end of the war US bombers dropped huge numbers of firebombs on Japanese cities and these, rather than fear of atomic bombs, led the civilian populations to seek shelter in the mountains.

'Two days later we arrived at a village. Some kind Russians fed us. They told us that Japan had lost. However, shooting still went on. That day the children and I came under fire near the Erdao River. We crouched by the bridge until evening darkness. When I took the baby, Kunio, from my oldest son's back, where he had been strapped, I found he had died. Not wanting to leave him in enemy territory, I lowered him into the river. It took a long time for me to let him go.

'On and on we went, for I cannot remember how many days, walking along railroad tracks. We met some Japanese soldiers on horseback. They told us that Japan had surrendered. You can imagine our feelings. And so we became prisoners of war. The Russians were kind to us. We moved to Hailin Prison Camp but the long ordeal had ended the short six-year life of Saio, my second son. No sooner had we buried him than we set out for another camp. My son Takashi was on my back. My oldest son held my hand. We reached camp at five in the evening. Takashi cried for water. Other prisoners had reached the camp before us. They gave us balls of steamed rice and water but Takashi died. It was 13 September. My own eyesight was failing. My skin was purplish black. Four days later my oldest son said; "I will never see Japan again" and died. Now, thirty-five years later, I am in Japan. The misery and pain of losing five small children and my husband to the cruelty of war tears at my heart.'[5]

Captured Japanese soldiers are led, barefoot and blindfolded, by their Chinese captors. As well as soldiers there were many Japanese civilians in Manchuria, the part of China Japan occupied. When the war ended these civilians became refugees stranded far from home.

Coping with shortages

At some time during the war, every country had to cope with shortages of food and other goods. Because women were usually the ones who ran the home, they had to cope with feeding and clothing families in spite of these shortages.

The USA was the richest country in the world. Despite the Depression just before the war, there were 27 million cars in the USA. Americans were used to owning refrigerators, toasters and washing machines, and having central heating. These were unheard-of luxuries for most women in the rest of the world.

When Japan attacked the US navy base at Pearl Harbor in Hawaii, in December 1941, there was war. America had to make tanks instead of cars, guns instead of washing machines. Before long women were back to doing hand washing, because there were no spare parts to mend their machines. Some goods became immediately unavailable because they were imported. The Japanese conquered Malaya where rubber came from: very soon there was no rubber for car tyres, shoe soles or anything else.

Save waste fats for explosives

TAKE THEM TO YOUR MEAT DEALER

This US poster encouraged women to save cooking fats for use in explosives. People everywhere were encouraged to save things such as aluminium pots and pans to make aeroplanes.

13

Women sewing parachutes made from nylon, which before the war would possibly have been used to make women's stockings.

Sugar, ships and stockings

Other goods were in short supply. Sugar and coffee were imported in ships, which were now needed to transport war goods. So sugar and coffee were rationed. Nylon was used to make parachutes. It took the equivalent of 36 pairs of nylon stockings to make one parachute, so nylon stockings almost disappeared from the shops. Women had to go back to wearing cotton and rayon stockings. Then rayon was used in tyre making and cotton for army uniforms so all stockings became scarce. As in Britain, women used leg makeup and even painted a pretend seam of the stocking up the backs of their legs.

Girdles and Bulges

Women's clothes were dealt a series of blows. Full or pleated skirts were banned, and so were patch pockets because they used too much material. Long dresses and

A spiv (illegal trader) selling nylon stockings. Because nylon was needed to make parachutes during the war, nylon stockings were rare and fetched a high price on the black market (see page 16).

large hats disappeared. Leather was needed for soldiers' boots so shoes became more scarce.

Women were used to wearing girdles to make themselves look slimmer. These were made with elasticated rubber. The rubber shortage meant that girdles were banned. Hands were raised in horror. There were two possibilities. One was to stay slim: magazines suggested cutting down on eating fats and sugars. The other was to wear looser clothing. Dress manufacturers helped with new designs. One advertisement ran: *'No girdle required for this dress of tobacco brown spun rayon with no fastenings (zippers gone to war) adjustable at waist and bust'* [6]

BRITAIN

Feeding a British family required patience in queueing and willingness to try new foods: *'Nettles can be used as a vegetable, for nettle tea and soup. The young shoots are tender. It is advisable NOT to use the coarse large leaves'* [7]

Women had to be persuasive enough to get the family to eat odd foods: *'Jam was one thing, elderberries in cakes instead of currants was one thing, potato pie, mashed potato sandwiches, fatless pastry and sugarless puddings all right, but my family drew the line at whale meat and tripe. They were never hungry enough for that.'* (Mary Livey from London, speaking to the author.)

A food queue in London during the war. Different kinds of food were used during wartime, and it often needed a lot of persuasion to get the family to eat such meals as tripe or whalemeat.

15

This German woman is cooking for her children on the most basic of stoves – a fire in the street. The picture was taken after the German surrender, when there was a terrible shortage of food throughout Germany.

GERMANY

In Germany rationing was introduced in 1939 and women were encouraged to have an *Eintopf* (one-pot) meal for at least one Sunday a month. This was a cheap, nourishing stew. As the war went on stews with less and less meat in them became more common. Even with rationing it was difficult to obtain such things as milk. By 1941 full cream milk was only allowed to pregnant women and sick people with a permit. An old woman in black came into a dairy near where an American worked, to beg for some milk for her son. *'You don't know how it is,'* she said in a low voice. *'They brought my son home yesterday in an ambulance.'* Wearily the shopkeeper said he could not give her milk. He heard such stories all day long. *'They brought him home with both his hands gone. Blown right off they told me. He can't eat anything and you give me skimmed milk.'* she cried quietly. The American offered his ration card. The shopkeeper declined and gave her the milk but he risked prosecution for doing it.

THE USSR

In the USSR rations were very low; sometimes as low as 100 grammes of potatoes and a cupful of grain for a person working a long day. Practically all the machines had been taken from the farms by the army, the oxen had been eaten and the horses were used for transport. Women were harnessed to ploughs half a dozen at a time to keep the farms going. Not a single tractor was delivered to any Soviet farm in 1941 and 1942.

THE BLACK MARKET

A black market flourished in most countries. The black market was made up of goods that were bought and sold without rationing. It was estimated that twenty per cent of the meat in the USA was on the black market. Because black market goods were illegal and scarce they were very expensive, and some dealers made a lot of money. In Britain nylon stockings fetched five shillings (25p) a pair: even today they cost only £1.00. The stockings were often sold by 'spivs' in markets or on street corners.

In Germany by the end of the war the black market was very large. Hiltegunt Zassenhaus lived with her widowed mother in Hamburg. Because the bombing had ruined so many homes they had three people staying in their house. One was a shady character who disappeared at night and returned with mysterious parcels. He was a dealer on the black market. Maybe much of what he got was stolen. It was difficult to survive in Europe without buying on the black market.

CHINA

There were some places that not even the black market could help. In China there was little food due to the long war against Japan. Parts of China were near famine by 1943 when countless thousands died of starvation. Gladys Aylward was a Christian missionary in China during the Japanese invasion and the war. She led a hundred children on an escape from the invading Japanese, across the Yellow River. Sometimes the Japanese were close. The fighting made food scarce.

Singapore

By 1943 Singapore, occupied by the Japanese, was suffering from all sorts of shortages because the Allies were sinking Japanese ships. Often shelves in the food shops were empty. Tapioca was grown in Singapore and began to be used for everything from cakes to pastry and bread. Some people kept chickens, but it was difficult to find food for them: 'We kept 20 or 30 fowls, but we had to look for something to feed them all the time. So we used to go down the drains with a candle to look for cockroaches.'[8]

A painting of Chinese people fleeing as the Japanese invaded China.

War Work – men's work

SHOULD WOMEN WORK?

Really there were a number of questions. What sort of work should women do? Would they need special looking after? Should they get paid as much as men? Would they distract men in the factories? Would they be willing to return to the home at the end of the war? All these questions were swept aside in the desperate need for more people to work in the factories. The government needed to replace the men who had gone to fight.

The US government started an advertising campaign to bring women into the factories.

Women worked in many industries. Notice the tightly tied scarf to protect her hair from being caught in the machinery.

Millionen deutscher Frauen und Mädchen arbeiten in Fabriken, Werkstätten und Büros ··· Es ist nicht unrecht, wenn wir verlangen, dass sich diese Millionen deutscher schaffender Volksgenossinnen noch viele Hunderttausende andere zum Vorbild nehmen
Adolf Hitler 4. Mai 1941

Deutsche Frau! Hilf mit

A poster calling on German women to help the war effort.

One slogan read: *'If you've followed recipes exactly for making cakes, you can learn to load shell.'* Women could, and did: in the USA, Britain, Germany and Russia, women became steel workers, welders, crane operators, rivetters, aeroplane engineers and munitions workers, to name just a few jobs.

BRITAIN AND THE USA

By the end of 1941, Britain made war work compulsory for unmarried women. A woman could choose between the women's armed services (army etc.), Civil Defence and industry. Women up to forty years of age had to register for war work and might be called up unless they had children under fourteen years of age. By 1943 7.5 million women were in paid work. This made up a third of the whole workforce. Women made up a third of the workforce in the USA by 1945.

Despite having different backgrounds and ways of life, women often had similar feelings about the work. Kitty Murphy worked at Woolwich Arsenal: *'I was putting the caps on the detonators of bullets. It was dangerous and you had to wear special clothing. We used to work seven till seven on days and seven till seven nights, seven days a week. But it was very good money. I was earning £10 a week with the danger money. I'd never been so well off.'*[9]

American women workers
Women made up about 12 per cent of the work force in shipyards and 40 per cent in aircraft assembly plants. They were popular workers in ordnance plants; in many they made up more than half the work force. In other industries percentages were higher – in one barrage balloon factory more than 90 per cent of the workers were women.

Women in the USA felt the same: they liked the money and the independence. Many black women had worked as servants before the war. Now they were needed in the factories and they liked the freedom. But freedom could mean loneliness. Some women left home for the first time and went to work kilometres away. Sometimes they lived in hostels. Many felt very homesick.

GERMANY
In 1939, most of Germany's 14 million working women were unpaid workers on family farms or did the worst-paid jobs in factories. When the war started and men went to fight, some women took over their husband's

A Soviet propaganda poster shows the part played by women in the rebuilding of Leningrad, which had been destroyed by the fierce fighting that raged around it during the war.

jobs and ran post offices and businesses. But on the whole the Nazi government in Germany encouraged the traditional view that women should stay at home: *'The female bird pretties herself for her mate and hatches the eggs for him. The man wards off the enemy.'* Joseph Goebbels, Nazi Propaganda Minister.

By 1941 the Nazis had to think again. Seven million men were in the armed services. The government launched a recruiting drive but few women were interested in factory work. In 1943 war work was made compulsory. The government said that all Germany was a woman's home and called up three million women between the ages of 17 and 45. Many did not go, because they had young children to look after. The same thing happened in all countries: governments (run by men) were slow to realize that women with young children could not just leave them all day. By the end of the war Britain, the USA and Germany were providing some nurseries, but nowhere near the number that were needed.

WOMEN AND SELF WORTH

Once at work in the factories German women proved to be as competent as their British and US counterparts. They were good at wiring ignition systems in Messerschmitt fighter planes or rivetting the fuselages of bombers. Only in Japan did the government find that at first women were not good at men's skilled jobs in factories. One government minister explained that Japanese women had always been told that they were inferior to men, so they did not believe that they could do men's jobs. Women had to be taught self worth, then they would believe in themselves and work as well as women in the West. In the end they did. As the war went on the Japanese situation became more desperate. By the summer of 1943 the government slogan was: *'Men to the Front. Women to the workplace.'* This was a great change for women. They drove buses, became barbers, clerks and sales people. They worked longer and longer hours in factories until

By 1945 German towns such as Frankfurt were in the front line as the Allies advanced. Everyone, women and children included, was called on to defend the Fatherland (Germany).

Soviet shortages

Soviet women struggled between home, factory, air raid post, digging defensive trenches and coping with rationing. Bread was rationed: 1.2 kilos a day for miners and other workers in heavy industry, industrial workers had 500 grammes a day, everyone else 400 grammes. Housewives had to go shopping at the peasant *kolkhoz* markets, where a litre of milk cost 38 roubles (it had cost 2 roubles in 1940). Other prices had gone up in the same way.

it was not worth going home. They slept on the floor as the next shift worked the machines. Hiroko Nakamoto remembered: '*On the night shift, after standing up for hours, we were marched into a dining hall where we had our supper. Supper was a bowl of weak, hot broth, usually with one string of noodle in it and a few soybeans in the bottom. We would gulp it down, then go back to work.*'[10]

It is clear that women did all sorts of men's jobs. It is also clear that they did not get paid the same money as men for the same job. In Japan women were seldom paid more than half a man's wages. Women at the Rolls Royce factory in Britain found they were doing skilled work, sometimes even training men in welding or doing precision work, and getting paid less than male lavatory cleaners. In 1943 the women went on strike and managed to get paid the same as semi-skilled men. They never got equality.

Did women become man-like? The thought of this scared a lot of men. Certainly women started to wear trousers to work. One German officer ordered his soldiers never to go out with '*trouser women*'. Some American films warned women what the consequences of taking men's jobs could be: in the 1942 musical, *Priorities on Parade*, a girl welder fell in love with a boy, but he was put off by her manly work. All ended happily however, when he discovered how pretty and feminine she was when she put down her welding gear and put on a dress.

Were women willing to return to the home at the end of the war? All over the world women seem to have been torn between love of their newfound independence and their desire to make a home and settle down far from the horrors of war. When the war ended, the desire to rebuild homes, find loved ones and forget the war often overrode the desire for independence. This seems particularly so in places like the USSR and Japan where the people on the home front had suffered so much.

A woman practising parachute jumping.

War work – women's work

Bringing up children, looking after people, and gathering, preparing and preserving food have been a huge part of women's work for thousands of years. It is not surprising, therefore, that women teaching, nursing and farming raised few eyebrows during the war (unlike engineering and flying aeroplanes).

TEACHERS AND NURSES

In Britain from early in the war onwards, women teachers and nurses no longer legally had to leave their jobs when they married. There was a great need for teachers as men went to fight, and an even greater need for nurses as the war continued. It was the same story in all the fighting countries. Japan called up women as both nurses and doctors.

Hiroko Kanazawa was called up in 1937 during the war with China: 'I was first assigned to the beautiful hospital ship Kasagi-maru which had a broad green stripe along its sides and flew the Red Cross flag. On this little ship we made more than 30 round trips between various places in Japan and ports in north China. The staff was divided into two groups. In each there were three head nurses and 27 ordinary nurses. There was one military doctor, two Red Cross doctors and one pharmacist. We carried 150 wounded soldiers on each trip.

'As long as your side is winning, the horror of war seems far removed. Radio news broadcast of one Japanese victory after another made our patients forget their suffering.'[11] Later Hiroko, like nurses from many of the fighting nations, was much closer to the front line.

A woman rescues a child from the rubble in London in 1944. Women worked as air raid wardens all through the war in both Britain and other countries.

23

Members of the Land Army in Britain. Many women went to work on farms, to take the place of men who had joined the army and gone away to fight.

In the USSR, women served as medical helpers on the battlefield. This required physical strength as well as knowledge of first aid. One Soviet officer trying to persuade a woman not to volunteer for the front line pointed out that nursing there involved dragging men from burning tanks. In many European countries and in the Far East, nurses were in the front line because bombing made home into a front line. Fire-bomb raids on Tokyo and other Japanese cities meant that nurses were working constantly with civilians as well as soldiers. After the atomic bomb was dropped on Hiroshima one of the many difficulties was that most of the nurses in the city had been killed.

FARMING

Soldiers and civilians need food. So farming was very important. Everywhere women took over their husband's and son's farms or went to work on other farms. In Germany in 1939, the National Labour Service programme meant that many 17- to 25-year-old girls worked on a farm for a year. They lived in barracks or local houses. Melita Maschmann remembered: *'It was a house like one in a child's painting. There were cushions of moss on the steeply pitched thatched roof,'* but the work was hard, *'I rubbed my hands raw doing the camp laundry and strained my back planting potatoes.'*[12]

In the USSR farming was less organized because of the German invasion. Whole villages were wiped out. Survivors such as Antonina Mironove fled from the

German tanks: '*The journey to Oblivskaya village took five days on foot. Then we went on to Stalingrad by locomotive. From Stalingrad by steamer and train to Medveditskoye and after five days waiting, by lorry to Frank. The Chairman of the May 1 Collective Farm looked gloomy sitting in his office. The burden of running the farm was on his shoulders. He only had women, children and old men. Some had no shoes and came from the towns. Unharvested fields of sunflowers and unstacked hay lay under the snow. He looked at the girls in front of him.*

'"*What can you do?*"

'"*I can drive a tractor if I'm taught how," I said.*

'*The tractors stood immobilized, covered by snow drifts and had to be dug out. We took them to pieces . . . My working day was totally dependent on the tractor. As long as it worked I didn't get off. Sometimes this meant 24 hours operation.*'[13]

Britain was not invaded but the need to produce food was still desperate. In 1939, two-thirds of the food the British ate was imported. This food came from all over the world in ships. Once war was declared the German submarines could easily sink these ships, so it was vital that Britain grew more food.

In the Soviet Union, the demand for guns was so urgent that they left the factory unpainted. As they were being trundled by rail to the war zone the guns were painted by a special women's brigade. In one giant tank factory of 8,500 workers, many women lived in holes in the ground. The punishment for absenteeism in the Soviet Union could be up to eight years in prison.

A woman in charge of a tractor. Before the Second World War it would have been unusual for a woman to do such a job in Western countries.

25

Digging up the back garden to grow vegetables to feed the family. This was part of a British campaign named 'Dig for Victory'.

The government put up posters to encourage people to grow vegetables and keep hens in their back gardens. But it was on farmers that the main burden of growing more food fell: to help them the Women's Land Army was started. By the end of the war there were over 80,000 women wearing the uniform of the Land Army. Many of them came from the towns. They found the work strange at first: '*Each time I cleaned out the pigs, I brought my breakfast up. But I soon got over that . . . I changed jobs several times between milking and general farm work on small and large farms. Then I worked with a gang of four girls going round Wiltshire farms with a steam-engine and threshing tackle.*'[14] Joan Shakesheff thought, '*Hedging and ditching was the worst – up to your knees in water most of the time. But muck-spreading, which sounds a terrible job, was a lovely job in the winter because you really got warm.*'[15]

These women were paid, but many women helped for nothing. In Britain the Women's Voluntary Service was started. It was the largest of the women's services: by 1944 it had a million members. Women did everything from knitting socks for seamen to running nurseries, collecting scrap metal and running rest centres for people who had been bombed out of their homes.

ENTERTAINMENT

Other women who had a different war experience were those who provided entertainment. This ranged from film stars to dancers and singers in clubs, from the famous like Vera Lynn to unknown singers entertaining soldiers on the Russian front.

Soviet entertainers

Soviet singers, musicians, dancers, actors and writers became involved, usually deeply involved, in the war effort. Many felt that their art was a weapon that could be used to encourage and sustain soldiers, the wounded and war workers. Ballet dancers danced in theatres for soldier audiences. Actresses and actors performed plays in settings such as tents, trenches, barns and even used a tank as a stage, looming high above the soldiers encircling it.

Women in combat

Should women fight and kill? This was the question that hung over calling women to fight in the Second World War.

QUASI-COMBATANT

In the USA and Britain the line was drawn firmly. Women could enter the armed services – drive lorries and ambulances, do desk jobs, cook, operate barrage balloons, work on decoding, be air raid wardens, deliver aeroplanes and 'man' anti-aircraft gun sites. But the aeroplanes they flew from factories to airfields could not have guns on them. And of the eight jobs on an anti-aircraft site, women could only do seven: they were never allowed to fire the gun.

Members of the French resistance forces during the liberation of Paris in 1944. Women played important roles in resistance movements all over the world.

A Soviet propaganda poster says 'Death – the German Way of Life'. An armed woman represents the Soviet state which is battling against the Germans. Women played a greater part in combat in the USSR than anywhere else.

СМЕРТЬ НЕМЕЦКИМ ОККУПАНТАМ!

WHEN THE FIGHTING WAS DESPERATE

On looking at women all around the world, it is easy to see that attitudes to women fighting were mainly shaped by the situation. Britain was more in the front line than the USA, but neither mainland country was ever invaded, so the women there did not have to fight. In Japan the attitude to women's role in fighting changed as the war went on. By the end, when the Japanese expected a US invasion, women were being armed and drilled to fight to the death. They were only armed with bamboo spears (shortages meant there were no other weapons available for them).

France, Poland and Italy were all invaded and women fought in the resistance movements. Often they carried guns, although sometimes men were opposed to it.

USSR AND THE GREAT PATRIOTIC WAR

In the USSR, the Second World War was known as the Great Patriotic War. There was less opposition there to women fighting. Perhaps this was partly because life for many Soviet citizens had always been hard and the hardship had been shared between women and men. Perhaps too, the tradition of the Communist Revolution in Russia in 1917 had given an ideal that women and men were equal. However, the overwhelming reason was probably that vast areas of the Soviet Union were invaded by the Germans. Every able-bodied person was needed to fight back.

The scale of the invasion and the suffering it caused is difficult to understand. It is now known that 20 million Russians died in the war. Whole villages and towns were burnt down. In Belorussia for example, every fourth Belorussian was burnt alive or killed by the invading Germans. As a result 60,000 Belorussian women fought in special resistance units. All in all 800,000 women served at the battle fronts.

Soviet women pilots

A few young Soviet women learned to fly at flying

ДА ЗДРАВСТВУЕТ XXV ГОДОВЩИНА
ЛЕНИНСКО-СТАЛИНСКОГО КОМСОМОЛА!

A 1943 poster encouraging the Soviet people to fight on. It shows Soviet women in uniform in the front line in 1943, just as they had been at the forefront of the revolution in 1918.

clubs before the war. Many had to join by the backdoor, working as waitresses in the clubs and then talking their way into having lessons. One outstanding flyer was Marina Raskova. When the war came she had so many letters from young Soviet girls who wanted to become flyers that she persuaded the airforce that she should form three women's air regiments. There was one fighter regiment (the 586th), one day bomber regiment (the 587th) and one night bomber regiment (the 588th).

The first fighter planes flown by Soviet women went into battle in April 1942, followed shortly by the bombers. The night bombers became the most famous planes flown by women: they were U-2 night bombers,

Ordinary jobs in the army

By the end of the war there were hundreds of women in every army division. Many, as in the American and British armies, did support jobs: women were drivers, office workers, paymasters, couriers, radar operators, code breakers and so on. Other mundane jobs had to be done too. For instance, the laundry for the twelve million strong Soviet army was done by huge detachments of women soldiers. They worked with the noise of the battlefield all around them, washing millions of uniforms.

which were primitive and slow with no special navigational equipment. They were too vulnerable for day flying. However, in the hands of good pilots, the slow speed and ability to fly very low helped precision bombing at night. It was not long before the women were very good, disciplined pilots. They learnt to go up to a high altitude and approach silently with the engine turned off. Gliding down and manoeuvring carefully they kept out of the way of enemy fighter planes. The planes carried eight bombs. (They could carry an extra 20kg of bombs because none of the three airwomen on board wore parachutes until it was made compulsory in 1944.) The Germans called these women nightwitches. They knew the flyers were female because they could hear the women singing just above them, as they glided in over the German lines before they dropped the bombs.

Summer 1942

There were fierce battles on the Southern Front: the Germans were pushing towards Stalingrad and the Caucasus Mountains. Over half the German army was on the Russian front. The airwomen and men flew sortie after sortie all night, bombing German rail and motor transport. They flew daytimes as well and slept anywhere – under the aircraft wing or in a haystack.

Members of the Soviet 46th bomber regiment at a briefing before a sortie in 1945. By then the war was almost over; for three years there had been Soviet women flying combat planes.

Falling back to the foothills of the Caucasus Mountains, the Soviets held the Germans back. The bombing regiment stayed in one place for several months. The difficult flying in the misty, turbulent air over the mountains and the constant missions to bomb bridges and keep the enemy back made excellent aircrews. Soon they were fully capable of enduring 'maximum' nights, with 15 or more sorties made by each aircrew. At night a mechanic had about five minutes to prepare each aircraft for flight. In the course of a night the armourers loaded up to four tonnes of bombs each.

By 1943 the German armies were being forced back. The bombers moved westwards as the Soviet army slowly advanced across its own devastated land, towards Germany. Many airwomen lost their lives: so did women in the Soviet army fighting far below them.

Doctors, tank drivers and snipers

Forty-one per cent of the Soviet army's doctors were women. Nearly half the front-line medical workers were women. They not only brought the wounded in from the battlefield under fire; they brought in the weapons as well.

The first public execution of a Soviet partisan fighter as the Germans invaded the USSR in 1941.

How men felt about women fighting

'We were retreating. It was autumn and raining. And by the roadside, I saw a dead girl . . . She was a medical orderly, in her uniform . . . A lovely girl with a long braid [plait]. She was all covered with mud . . . The girl's presence among us and her death amidst all that horror, mud and chaos – it was all so unnatural. I saw many deaths but that one stuck in my memory.' (Nikolai Borisovich, in *War's Unwomanly Face*.)

31

A Soviet woman rescue worker helping a wounded soldier. As well as bringing the solder back to safety, she has managed to retrieve his gun.

The work was dangerous, as Nina Yakovlevna recalled: '*In tank units medical orderlies didn't last long. There was no place inside the tank for us. We clung to the armour and thought about only one thing: how to keep our feet clear of the caterpillar tracks. And all the time you had to watch if there were any tanks on fire. It was your job to get the tankmen out. There were five of us girls together. They were all killed except me.*'[16]

As the war went on and more men were killed, more women soldiers appeared in the front line. Women were thought to be very good snipers because they were very patient. Less dramatic but equally frightening were the duties of the woman sappers who cleared mines. Some women served as ordinary soldiers: despite their smaller size women carried wounded men back from the front. Women tank crews served mostly in medium-sized tanks: fewer served in heavy tanks. One exception was Junior Lieutenant Aleksandra Boiko, who became commander of an IS-122 heavy tank: her husband was the driver.

Invasion and resistance

Many countries were invaded. The Channel Islands (part of Britain) were invaded. There was little resistance because the islands were so small that there was nowhere for anyone to hide. On the whole the Germans treated the Channel Islanders reasonably. All through the war the islands were full of young German soldiers and inevitably there were romances with the local girls. Over 2,000 Anglo-German babies were born on the Channel Island called Jersey.

Jersey was not the only place where women had the children of 'enemy' soldiers. Many women fell in love with men who were supposed to be their enemies. Often the results were sad. Lisa was fifteen years old, the daughter of a German farmer. She fell in love with

'My mother has just died. I was her youngest and very close to her. She told me once of what happened to her in the war. She was Austrian and at the end of the war the Russians arrived. She was raped many times by the Russian soldiers and as a result she became pregnant. She got away to Berlin, to a relative. In those days, as the war was ending, conditions were very bad. Berlin was a ruin. There was very little food, no heating, nowhere warm to live. She had a baby boy; he seemed weak and had chest trouble. She had not wanted him and she just let him die although her aunt pleaded with her. Later she came to England, married and had five children. She never told anyone what had happened but she never forgave herself for letting the baby die.' (Recounted to the author in 1990).

French women at the end of the war with their heads shaved. In many occupied countries women had children whose fathers were members of the invading forces: they were often shunned or had their heads shaved, or worse, as a result.

33

Ivan, the Soviet prisoner of war working on her father's farm. They had sex and she became pregnant. Her father threw her out and sent Ivan away.

Unfortunately rape by soldiers of an invading army was more common than loving. Either way babies were born. Sometimes the women made sure the babies died in the turmoil and shortages of war, sometimes the babies were adopted, and sometimes they were accepted. Often the children and the women suffered: they were sneered at and not accepted.

ITALY

In 1943 Italy surrendered to the Allies but was immediately overrun by Germans. Women made up ten per cent of the resistance or partisan forces. Carla Capponi was a twenty-year-old translator and typist in Rome: *'Naturally the Germans didn't think that a woman could have carried a bomb so this became the women's task. Some, like me, set them off as well. But in many instances women were not given arms because men believed that they were more emotional and less capable of making decisions. When I first joined I had a gun of my father's but the other partisans took it from me. However, I was riding on the bus one day and happened to be standing close to a German soldier so I stole his gun, a Beretta sub-machine gun. That is how I regained a gun.'*

POLAND

Poland was overrun by Germany early in the war. It is not known how many Polish women helped in the resistance but the number probably runs into hundreds of thousands. There were certainly 40,000 in the Polish Home Army. There was one all-female regiment that operated in the forests of eastern Poland. There were 6,700 Polish women who escaped to Britain and helped the army.

Many other women stayed in Poland and resisted. Perhaps the most remarkable were the Girl Guides in Warsaw who scouted escape and supply routes through

Carla Capponi was an Italian resistance member who was assigned to assassinate a German officer outside his hotel: 'It was a traumatic experience. I almost wanted to call him, to make him turn around but I knew he was armed. It seemed impossible that I should hold the gun, point it at him and shoot him in the back. When I had done it I began running down the street with the gun in my hand. It was raining and tears were streaming down my face. Afterwards Rosario joined me and tried to calm me down. He told me that the first time he had to shoot a man he felt the same way.

'After getting over the initial shock, especially since many of our comrades were being arrested and tortured, all our scruples were replaced by determination to fight for our cause.'[17]

the city sewers, smuggled weapons and joined the armed uprising against the Germans in 1944. Ida was in her early twenties and was in charge of a unit of 30 women. They were responsible for carrying the wounded from street battles, carrying messages and delivering guns: *'We slept in the cellars of the houses. Parts of the city were completely cut off from each other. The worst thing for most of us was not knowing the fate of our families. The German planes flew so low that sometimes we could shoot them down with rifles. The city was on fire, rocked by explosions day and night. It took hours to go a kilometre or even a few blocks. Food shortages grew acute. A group of twenty prostitutes organized and began to help us. They went to an old brewery nearby and got heavy sacks of grain and delivered these all over our section of Warsaw.'*[18] The rising went on for 63 days but at last the Germans closed in and the Poles had to surrender. Many women were sent to concentration camps.

Some women never had the chance to resist. As Germany swept into the USSR, thousands of women were captured and deported to work on German and Polish farms. Those who survived spent the war underfed and working as slaves.

The end of the resistance in Warsaw after the uprising of 1944. These people wait to be taken to a concentration camp.

Internment and imprisonment

At the start of the war, fear of an invasion of the US West Coast led the US government to intern Japanese Americans. This little girl is waiting alone to be sent to an internment camp.

When war came life was difficult for foreigners living in their enemy's country. For instance, there were Germans and Italians living in Britain, Americans living in the Philippines and Japanese living in America. When the war began there was panic.

BRITAIN

In Britain, 30,000 enemy aliens were arrested in the summer of 1940 when it looked as though Germany was going to invade. Women were imprisoned separately from men. Several hundred spent weeks in prison before being sent to camps. There were all sorts: in Holloway prison in June 1940 there were a schoolgirl, a German nun who had been in an English convent for 20 years, a German teacher from an English school and two English women married to Germans (they had been visiting their families in England when war broke out). The terrible thing was that about half the internees were Germans who had fled from Nazi Germany and had come to Britain to be free. Some spent the war in camps surrounded by barbed wire, though many were released once the first panic was over.

INTERNMENT OF JAPANESE

After the Japanese attack on Pearl Harbor in December 1941, President Roosevelt ordered the evacuation of all US citizens from Japanese families who lived on the West Coast of the USA. It was feared that they would side with the Japanese forces. Men, women and children were all forced to leave their homes at very short notice, and women suddenly had to cope with the burdens of looking after a family while living in a detention camp in their own country.

THE PHILIPPINES

Far across the world in the Philippines a different internment took place. Natalie Crouter was American. She and her husband had lived comfortably in the Philippines, where he ran a business. When the war came the Japanese invaded the island and interned all the British and Americans. Natalie and her husband were forced to live in a camp together with 500 others.

Below The sinking of the USS Arizona, *part of the destruction brought by the Japanese attack on Pearl Harbor in December 1941. The attack on Pearl Harbor led to the USA joining the war, against Japan: thousands of Japanese Americans were interned soon afterwards.*

A US army nurse in the Philippines. Many US nurses travelled a great deal, as the US army fought in both Europe and the Pacific.

Work was divided into women's work (waitressing in the camp dining hall, babysitting, nursing, laundry) and men's work (wood chopping, running the machine shop, dealing with sanitation). Both sexes taught in the school. The Men's Committee had the complete power over all supplies (mattresses, firewood, medicines, food) over all decisions and rules for the camp. The women seem to have accepted this (though in her diary Natalie objects to having no say).

Natalie kept a diary that by the end of the war was 5,000 pages long. She wrote in tiny writing on little scraps of paper. Then she wrapped them in squares cut from an old raincoat and hid them. If the Japanese had found she kept a diary Natalie would have been killed. Much of her diary was about food. The rations were small – some vegetables and rice sweepings. The people in the camp pooled hidden stores of money to buy food, or were helped by their Filippino friends and ex-servants who guarded buried valuables and sold them to buy food for the internees. They also sent presents: '*March 21, 1942: Martha received a baby basket trimmed with ruffles by her Filippino girl* [servant] *on the outside.*

'*March 23, 1942: Inez sent me a large tin of delicious native coffee for the camp through me. I will not turn it over to the kitchen* (the kitchen group did very well for itself according to Natalie in other entries) *but will serve a pot of coffee to every group, each day. First, the toilet workers, next the towel washers, then the women vegetable cutters, then the British girls who get no packages and so on.*

'*July 11, 1942: A bag from Nida* (an ex-servant) *with raw pork chops, mangoes, toothpaste, chowchow pickle and pineapple. That girl is inspired. How do they manage to live themselves?'*

As the war went on everyone lived with greater and greater difficulty. Food became more and more scarce. Natalie became weak and ill. By 1945 they knew the war must be nearly over. The USA retook the Philippines on the way to defeat Japan. Natalie did not

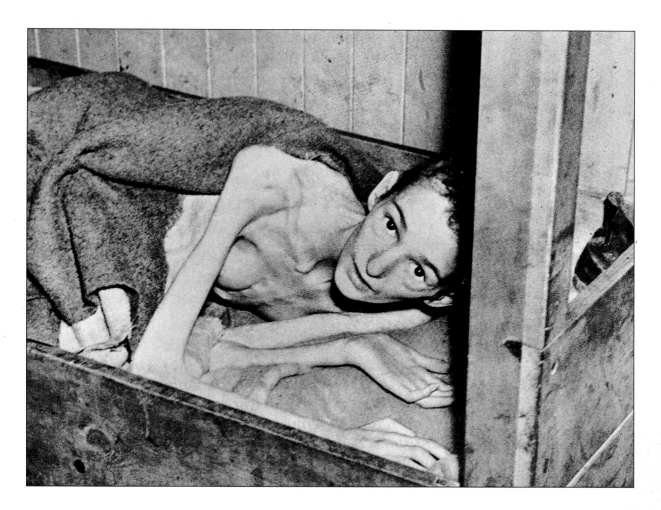

know whether to be glad or sorry. She knew she would have to go back to hospital in the USA, and felt in many ways that she was closer to her Japanese captors and the local Filippinos than she was to the Americans back home in the USA.

IMPRISONMENT

Jewish women, female resistance fighters and any other women who opposed Hitler's rule might be imprisoned in concentration camps or prisoner of war camps. After the Warsaw Uprising of August to October, 1944, 15,000 Polish resistance fighters who had held out for 63 days were sent to camps. Among them were 2,000 women and 550 children. Usually the conditions and treatment were terrible.

A woman in a German concentration camp. Jewish women, women who opposed Nazism, members of resistance movements and others were sent to the camps.

Peter Bielenberg was a German political prisoner in Ravensbruck concentration camp, which mainly contained women: ' . . . *under my window was a wall – some sort of punishment wall – and all day long in the bitter cold women who had been beaten until they could hardly stand were made to lean against that wall. My cell was never silent all day long, and sometimes at night I listened to the crying, the moaning and the whimpering of those beaten women – like animals in pain . . . there was one particular wardress – not a wardress really but an inmate who had been promoted to Camp police, "Kapos" they were called – never without a whip. One night I heard screams and thuds coming from the courtyard and then this bitch's voice talking – I couldn't stand it – "Stop that ruddy noise at once!" I yelled, hoping they would think it came from the guardroom next door to my cell. It seemed to work; I heard that Kapo creature say, "Pity, I would have liked to give her a few more" – the moaning stopped soon afterwards too. Then on Christmas Eve I was woken by a different sort of music, a choir from the camp singing Christmas carols. Beautiful voices* – Stille Nacht [Silent Night]. *They sang again on Christmas Day outside their barracks and believe it or not that Kapo bitch was leader of the choir – had a voice like a bell. But I also saw great deeds of courage under my window – women who came to comfort and bring water knowing they would be standing there themselves the next day.* [They were] *Bibelforscher* – Quakers I think you would call them – incredible courage.'[19]

When the Americans and British fought their way into Germany in 1945 they were shocked to find the concentration camps. They made the German guards bury the dead and clear up the camps. Many photographs were taken to show the world that this sort of brutality by men and women to other men and women must not happen again.

Conclusion

The Second World War ended in 1945. For everyone peace meant big changes in their lives. Both men and women found it difficult to settle down after the war. Marisa, who fought in the Italian resistance, highlighted one problem: *'Those first months were difficult. Getting back to normal wasn't easy. First of all, I think, it is very hard to live without a gun once you have had one.'*[20] Only a small proportion of women in Britain had carried guns, but by the end of the war there were 460,000 women in the armed services and over six and a half million in civilian war work. Most of them faced the ending of their jobs.

Vera Cole was in the ATS. Demobilization lists were put up: *'I saw my name and suddenly realized that my days in the ATS were fast coming to an end . . . Before I left, an officer whom I had never seen before called me over and gave me my conduct sheet on which was written "exemplary", thanked me, wished me well and said goodbye . . . I was out, services no longer required.'*[21]

For most women it was back to the home and coping with the continuing shortages that a long and destructive war had brought about. In the USA and Canada this made life a little harder than before the war but still much more glamorous than in Europe.

This 1942 poster, asking women to save old clothes to be made into uniforms, shows a woman's place as in the home rather than at work. At the end of the war many women found that the jobs they had done during the war were required for men returning from the fighting.

Towards the end of the war there were thousands of US and Canadian soldiers in Britain. They had more money, better uniforms, more food and so on than the British servicemen. There were many romances with British girls: some lasted and some didn't. Jessie Robins was living in a Devon village when the Americans arrived. She fell in love with a US army sergeant. By June 1944 she was pregnant: '*We used to talk about our future together and what would happen after the war and it seemed quite natural to sleep with him. I thought I was going to America, he told me he wanted to take me, and I didn't think it was a dreadful thing to do. One Sunday morning, one of my friends came running up and said, did I know they were all leaving? I left everything and ran all the way to the village. The convoy was getting ready. Jack, being a sergeant, was waving men on to lorries and looking up the road for me. He said, "We're going now" – the most terrible moment of my life, I think. He kept saying, "Don't worry." He wrote to me often and sent money for my daughter, but he never came back.*'[22]

Some girls did marry GIs (American soldiers), and whole shiploads of GI brides sailed off to the USA and Canada when the war ended. For some it worked well. Some took one look and caught the next boat home. Others made the best of a different life. Often they were girls who had been in the services and were suddenly in small towns, having to fit in with their

GI brides (British women who had married US soldiers) waving goodbye before sailing for the USA in 1946.

*Clearing away the ruins of
the bombed city of Essen.
The women had to clear
rubble for 90 days to
qualify for a ration card.*

husband's family whom they had never met. They had
lovely homes by British standards, but little to do. The
women were far from families and friends, and often
met resentment because the husband had been
expected to marry a local girl.

In Britain, rationing and shortages continued. For
many women the end of the war was a great relief.
Men came home and women could pick up the threads
of ordinary life again, but it wasn't easy. The divorce
rate rose: some people found it difficult to adjust when
they had been apart for a long time. Others had made
hasty marriages in the war and regretted them.

In other parts of Europe, shortages were more severe.
In the Soviet Union, Nadya went home: *'We had
dreamed of victory for four years. Here it was, but not
our dreams of returning to a good night's sleep on
clean sheets. We came home to face all the destruction
and severe food shortages. We worked eighteen hours
a day to reconstruct. Maybe that is why we didn't have
much post-combat stress – we didn't have time to
reflect on our personal experiences in the war, we
were too occupied by the present. Most of us got
married and began to have children. Only later would I
sit and think of our regiment, of the closeness we
shared. The amazing thing is that the close friendships
remained. Every year, at least once a year, we have
reunions.'*[23]

Many women, however busy they became with everyday life and families, missed the close companionship and missed their comrades. Brigitte was a French resistance fighter who spent fourteeen months in a concentration camp and nearly died. Her experience of returning home was like many women's, only more extreme: '*Returning from hell, I felt so old. We got back to civilization and we were not understood. We were like people coming from the moon. I was so different. I was not like my family any more. I was like my fellow deportees.*'[24] Brigitte went on to become a war correspondent, obsessed with death and feeling that only her war companions understood her. She was fascinated by analysing war's causes and effects. As a war correspondent, she could watch war bringing out both the worst and the best in human beings.

Perhaps that is the one uniting thread for all women's experiences in the Second World War, anywhere in the world. War does not leave any room for frivolities like which television programme to watch, which pair of shoes to buy or where to go on holiday. Instead, war concentrates the mind on the necessities of survival.

Office workers cheering at the news that the war had ended. At the war's end many thousands of women had learned that they could be mechanics, intelligence officers, farmworkers, pilots, assassins and a hundred other things besides. They were soon to find that returning soldiers did not want to compete with women for jobs, and that they were expected to return to their old work in the home.

Timeline

1929   *October*   29th Wall Street Crash leads to Great Depression.

1931   *April*   14th Spain becomes a republic.

1933   *January*   30th Hitler appointed Chancellor of Germany. *August*   2nd Hitler made Fuhrer.

1935   *October*   2nd Italian troops invade Ethiopia.

1936   *February*   Popular Front wins elections in Spain. *March*   8th German troops enter Rhineland. *July* 18th Spanish Civil War begins. *November*   1st Rome-Berlin Axis signed between Italy and Germany.

1937   *July*   7th Japan attacks China. *November*   6th Italy, Germany and Japan unite in Anti-Comintern Pact.

1938   *March*   12th Anschluss (union) of Austria and Germany begins. *August-Sept.*   International confrontation over Hitler's demands for part of Czechoslovakia (Sudetenland). *Sept.*   30th Munich Conference resolves Czechoslovakian crisis. *October*   12th German troops enter Sudetenland.

1939   *March*   15th German forces occupy Czechoslovakia. 28th Franco's forces capture Madrid; Spanish Civil War ends. 31st France and Britain guarantee Polish independence. *May*   2nd Germany and Italy agree Pact of Steel. *August*   23rd USSR-German Non-aggression Pact. *September*   1st Germany invades western Poland. 3rd France and Britain declare war on Germany. 17th Soviet troops invade eastern Poland.

1940   *April*   7th Norway and Denmark attacked by Germany. *May*   10th German troops begin invasion of Netherlands, Belgium and Luxembourg. Chamberlain resigns; Churchill made British prime minister. 12th Germany begins invasion of France. *June* 10th Italy declares war on Britain and France. 14th German forces capture Paris. 22nd French sign armistice at Compiegne. Battle of Britain starts. *Sept.*   27th Germany, Italy and Japan sign Tripartite Pact. *November*   5th Roosevelt re-elected US President. 14th Coventry levelled by German bombers.

1941   *March* 11th US Lend-Lease Act signed. *April*   17th Germany launches invasion of Balkans and Greece. *June*   22nd Operation Barbarossa (invasion of USSR) begun by Germany. *July*   USA launches embargoes on oil and steel exports to Japan. *August*   14th Roosevelt and Churchill sign Atlantic Charter, agreeing war aims. *November*   German forces halted outside Moscow. *December*   7th Japan bombs US naval base at Pearl Harbour, Hawaii. Japan declares war on USA.

8th USA and Britain declare war on Japan. 11th Germany and Italy declare war on USA; USA declares war on them.

1942   *February*   15th Singapore captured by Japanese. *April*   9th US forces on Bataan Peninsula surrender. *May*   6th US forces on Corregidor surrender. *July*   Battle of Stalingrad begins. *November*   8th US and British forces land in North Africa. 11th German forces enter Vichy, France.

1943   *January*   14-24th Casablanca Conference agrees Allied war aim of unconditional surrender. *February*   2nd German army at Stalingrad surrenders. *May*   12th War ends in North Africa. *July*   10th Allied forces land in Sicily. 26th Mussolini resigns. *September*   3rd Allies land in Italy. 8th Italy surrenders to Allies. 10th Nazis occupy Rome. *November*   22-25th Cairo Conference. 28th Tehran Conference opens.

1944   *March* Soviet troops enter Poland. *June*   4th US and British troops enter Rome. 6th D-Day; Allied invasion of France begins. *July*   20th Hitler wounded in assassination attempt by senior German officers. 21st Dumbarton Oaks Conference lays down basis for United Nations. *August*   Warsaw Uprising begins. 25th Paris liberated. *October*   Warsaw Uprising crushed. 6th Soviet forces enter Hungary and Czechoslovakia. 20th US forces enter Philippines. *November*   All-out US bombing of Japan begins. *December*   16th German forces launch attack through Ardennes in Belgium.

1945   *February*   4th Yalta Conference. *April*   1st US forces occupy Okinawa. 12th Roosevelt dies. 20th Soviet forces enter Berlin. 28th Mussolini executed. *May* 1st Hitler's suicide announced in Berlin. 2nd Berlin falls. 7th Germany signs unconditional surrender. *June*   26th UN formed. *July*   17th Potsdam Conference opens. *August*   6th Atomic bomb dropped on Hiroshima. 8th Atomic bomb dropped on Nagasaki. *September*   2nd Japan signs surrender.

1946   *March*   5th Churchill's 'Iron Curtain' speech.

1947   *March*   12th Truman Doctrine outlined. *June*   5th Marshall Plan put forward.

1948   *June*   24th USSR begins blockade of West Berlin (ends 12 May 1949).

Glossary

Absentee   A person who is away from work for some reason.

Alien   A person or thing from another place. During the war, people whose families had come from a nation on the other side were known as enemy aliens.

Armourer   A person who loads bombs and bullets.

ATS   (British) Auxiliary Territorial Service. The women of the ATS provided support for soldiers by, for example, cooking for them, doing their washing or putting on shows.

Autobiography   A book written by someone about her or his life.

Barracks   A building in which soldiers live.

Black market   Not an actual market with stalls, but a name for the unofficial trade in goods that are hard to get hold of elsewhere. Black market goods are more expensive than they would be in shops.

Civil Defence   A British non-military organization that tried to help people protect themselves against bombing raids.

Convoy   A group of vehicles – for example ships or trucks – travelling together for protection.

Demobilization   Disbanding an army and sending people home.

Deportee   A person who has been sent away from a place – often a country – to live somewhere else.

Depression, the   A time of high unemployment and poverty in the USA during the early 1930s. The Depression spread from the USA to Europe and the rest of the world, because US banks suddenly needed back the money they had lent to businesses in other countries. Because these businesses could not repay the loans, they were forced to close.

Evacuation   The removal of people from a dangerous area.

Famine   A shortage of food over a large area.

Internment   During the Second World War, internment was the name given to the putting of enemy aliens (see separate entry under aliens) into places that they could not leave.

Land Army   A British organization of women who worked on farms during the war.

Navigator   Someone who reads maps and decides where to go.

Ordnance factory   A factory in which guns and bombs are made.

Precision bombing   The careful bombing of a specific target.

Ration   A fixed portion, for example of meat, bread or milk.

Resistance   An organization of people fighting against the occupation of their country.

Scrap metal Metal that can be melted down and used to make something else.

Sniper A soldier who hides on her or his own and waits to shoot at the enemy.

Sortie A mission, usually in an aircraft, to attack the enemy.

Women's Voluntary Service An organization of women who did all sorts of jobs to help the war effort.

WRENS The Women's Royal Naval Service, part of the British Navy.

Books to read

Many of these books are really for older readers, but could be dipped into by younger people. Some will only be available in larger libraries.

War's Unwomanly Face, S Alexiyevich, Progress Publishers 1985. Contains interviews with women who fought in the war. Excellent to dip into: one of the few published works in English about Soviet fighting women.

The Past is Myself, Christabel Bielenberg, Chatto & Windus 1968. A classic book, and an excellent and moving read: hard to put down.

Hiroshima Maidens, Rodney Barker, Viking 1985. The story of 14 girls badly burnt in the dropping of the bomb on Hiroshima, taken to the USA for cosmetic surgery.

Women in War, Shelley Saywell, Costello, 1986. Good interviews with resistance fighters in France, Italy etc. The Second World War is covered from pp. 1-130.

Sources of quotations
1 and **1a** *The Day War Broke Out,* Marshall Cavendish 1989; **2** *One Woman's Army,* Charity Adams Earley, Texas A and M University Press, 1989; **3** *War's Unwomanly Face,* S Alexiyevich, Progress Publishers (Moscow) 1985; **4** *China in Peace and War,* Madame Chiang Kai-shek, Hurst and Blackett, 1940; **5** *Women Against War,* Women's Division of Soka Gakkai Peace Committee, Kodansha International Ltd 1986; **6** *Don't You Know There's a War On?* Richard Lingeman, GP Putnam 1980: **7** *Country Life* magazine; **8** Chu Shen Choo in *Singapore Under the Japanese 1942-45,* Singapore Heritage Society 1992; **9** *A People's War,* Peter Lewis, Methuen 1986; **10** *My Japan 1930-51,* Mildred Masten Place, McGraw Hill 1970; **11** *Women Against War;* **12** *Account Rendered,* Melita Maschmann, 1964; **13** *War's Unwomanly Face;* **14** *Love, Sex and War,* John Costello, Collins 1985; **15** *A People's War;* **16** *War's Unwomanly Face;* **17** and **18** *Women in War,* Shirley Saywell, Costello 1986; **19** *The Past is Myself,* Christabel Beilenburg, Chatto and Windus, 1968; **20** *Women in War;* **21** *Women Who Went to War,* Eric Taylor, Grafton 1989; **22** *A People's War;* **23** and **24** *Women in War.*

Index

This index is about things women did in the war, so the entry 'assassin' refers to a woman who was an assassin, the entry 'collaboration' refers to female collaborators, and so on. The numbers in bold refer to text that has a picture to go with it.